17∠

Baldwinsville Public Library
33 East Genesee Street
Baldwinsville, NY 13027-2575

DEC 1 2 2013

WITHDRAWN

D1207550

Machines at Work

Machines on a Construction Site

Baldwinsville Public Library
33 East Genesee Street
Baldwinsville, NY 13027-2575

Siân Smith

Heinemann
LIBRARY
Chicago, Illinois

© 2014 Heinemann Library
an imprint of Capstone Global Library, LLC
Chicago, Illinois

All rights reserved. No part of this publication may be
reproduced or transmitted in any form or by any means,
electronic or mechanical, including photocopying.

Edited by Dan Nunn and John-Paul Wilkins
Designed by Cynthia Akiyoshi
Picture research by Elizabeth Alexander
Production by Sophia Argyris
Originated by Capstone Global Library Ltd
Printed and bound in China by Leo Paper Products Ltd

17 16 15 14 13
10 9 8 7 6 5 4 3 2 DEC 1 2 2013

Library of Congress Cataloging-in-Publication Data
Cataloging-in-Publication data is available at the Library
of Congress: loc.gov

ISBN 978-1-4329-7500-5 (hardback)
ISBN 978-1-4329-7505-0 (paperback)

Acknowledgments
We would like to thank the following for permission
to reproduce photographs: Alamy pp. 7 (© Robert
Convery), 8 (© G P Bowater), 16 (© paul ridsdale), 19
(© Everyday Images), 23 grapple (© PhotoAlto); Getty
Images pp. title page (narvikk/Vetta), 14 (Creti Stefano/
Flickr); Shutterstock pp. 4, 23 construction site (© Yuriy
Chertok), 5, 11, 23 excavator (© Dmitry Kalinovsky),
9, 23 tracks (© Norman Bateman), 10 (© Toa55), 12
(© AlexKZ), 13, 23 dump box (© Johan Larson), 18 (©
David Hughes), 21 (© Rigucci), 22 (© marilyn barbone);
SuperStock pp. 6 (© Richard Heinzen/Purestock), 15,
23 cab (© Science Faction), 17 (© Reino Hannine/age
footstock), 20 (© Tetra Images).

Design element photographs of car engine part (©
fuyu liu), crane (© Nolte Lourens), gear cog (© Leremy),
and tire tread (© Robert J. Beyers II) reproduced with
permission of Shutterstock.

Front cover photograph of an excavator at a construction
site reproduced with permission of Getty Images
(narvikk/Vetta). Back cover photographs of a small
bulldozer (© Norman Bateman) and dump truck
(© Johan Larson) reproduced with permission
of Shutterstock.

We would like to thank Dee Reid and Marla Conn for
their invaluable help in the preparation of this book.

Every effort has been made to contact copyright holders
of material reproduced in this book. Any omissions will
be rectified in subsequent printings if notice is given to
the publisher.

All the Internet addresses (URLs) given in this book were
valid at the time of going to press. However, due to the
dynamic nature of the Internet, some addresses may
have changed, or sites may have changed or ceased to
exist since publication. While the author and publisher
regret any inconvenience this may cause readers, no
responsibility for any such changes can be accepted by
either the author or the publisher.

Contents

Some words are shown in bold, **like this**. You can
find out what they mean by looking in the glossary.

Why Are There Machines at a Construction Site?

A **construction site** is a place where things are built.

Builders could be making bridges, roads, houses, or other buildings.

There are many different jobs that need to be done at a construction site.

Machines make the jobs safer and easier to do.

Which Machines Help to Break Things Up?

Sometimes buildings have to be knocked down before new ones can be built.

Cranes swing heavy wrecking balls to knock buildings down.

crane

wrecking ball

drill

concrete

Sometimes construction workers need to break up the ground.

Powerful drills are used to break up hard concrete.

Which Machines Get the Ground Ready for Building?

A bulldozer has a large blade at the front. This is used to clear the ground.

Most bulldozers have **tracks** instead of wheels. This helps them to move on lumpy ground and mud.

blade

track

small bulldozer

Small bulldozers are also important.
They are useful because they can get
into small spaces.

A machine called a motor grader makes the ground smooth and ready to build on.

The long blade scrapes along the ground to make it flat.

blade

bucket

Wheel loaders are used to scoop up soil or rocks and carry them away.

The bucket at the front moves down to shovel things in, then lifts up to carry them.

Which Machines Carry Rocks, Soil, and Sand?

Wheel loaders often move rocks, soil, and sand into dump trucks.

Dump trucks are big and powerful enough to carry huge loads.

wheel loader

dump truck

dump box

The container or **dump box** can be lifted up so that the load tips out easily.

Most dump trucks tip out their loads at the back, but some tip at the sides.

What Are Digging Machines Used For?

Digging machines are very useful for construction work. They are also called backhoes or **excavators**.

The bucket can be used for many things, such as digging, loading, or carrying.

bucket

arm

cab

The bottom part of a digging machine holds it steady. The driver's **cab** and digging arm can move around in a circle.

The long arm on a digging machine lets it reach high and far, and dig down deep.

Can Digging Machines Do Other Jobs?

Different tools can be attached to a digging machine. Magnets or giant claws called **grapples** can be used to lift things up.

magnet

rock breaker

Other tools, such as saws, hammers, and rock breakers, can be put on a digging machine to break things up.

Drills can be put on a digging machine to make holes in the ground.

What Is a Backhoe Loader?

A backhoe loader is actually two different machines made into one.

The front of the machine is a wheel loader and the back is a digging machine. Can you tell which is which?

cab

The seat inside the **cab** turns around so that the driver can use both machines.

Backhoe loaders are used to do a lot of work at **construction sites**.

Which Machines Are Used to Reach High Places?

Buildings at a **construction site** can be very tall.

Machines with moving platforms called cherry pickers can lift builders up high.

tower crane

Cranes are used to move heavy materials up and down.

Cranes can be fixed to the ground or to trucks. Some cranes can be made taller, to match the height of a building.

What Does This Machine Do?

Can you guess what this **construction site** machine does?

Find the answer on page 24.

22

Picture Glossary

cab place where the driver sits

construction site place where things are built

dump box part on a dump truck that holds the load

excavator another name for a digging machine

grapple tool shaped like a claw. It is used for picking things up and holding them.

tracks long metal belt that a machine can move on instead of wheels

Find Out More

Books

Alexander, Heather. *Big Book of Construction Machines* (John Deere). New York: DK, 2009.

Harris, Nicholas. *A Year at a Construction Site* (Time Goes By). Minneapolis: Millbrook, 2009.

Internet Sites

Facthound offers a safe, fun way to find Internet sites related to this book. All of the sites on Facthound have been researched by our staff.

Here's all you do:
Visit www.facthound.com
Type in this code:
9781432975005

Index

The construction site machine on page 22 mixes cement.